To Joshua,

I hope that you will always continue to feel connected to the world of nature. With best wishes and hopes that you will always treasure the gifts of life.

Nancy Sohn Swartz

May 15, 2005

In Our Image

God's First Creatures

by Nancy Sohn Swartz
Illustrated by Melanie Hall

Library of Congress Cataloging-in-Publication Data
Swartz, Nancy Sohn, 1944–
In our image / by Nancy Sohn Swartz ; illustrated by Melanie Hall.
p.   cm.
Summary: When God asks the newly-created animals and all of creation to share their gifts with the human beings God is about to create, they respond generously.
ISBN 1-879045-99-0
1. Creation—Juvenile literature.
2. Man (Theology)—Juvenile literature. [1. Creation. 2. God.] I. Hall,
Melanie W., ill. II. Title.
BS651.S88 1998
296.3'2—dc21 97-38803
CIP
AC

10 9 8 7 6 5 4 3 2
Manufactured in the United States of America
Book and jacket designed by Delphine Keim Campbell
Text edited by Sarah Swartz

For People of All Faiths, All Backgrounds

Published by Jewish Lights Publishing
A Division of LongHill Partners, Inc.
Sunset Farm Offices, Route 4
P.O. Box 237
Woodstock, Vermont 05091
Tel: (802) 457-4000 Fax: (802) 457-4004
www.jewishlights.com

There are a number of people I wish to acknowledge. I would like to thank my husband Peter, my sons David, Michael, and Ray, and all the members of my family and friends for their support and encouragement. I thank Sandra Korinchak from Jewish Lights for believing in me and in my story. And I also thank Temple Beth Am of Randolph and Rabbi Loel Weiss for providing me with an atmosphere that nurtured my feelings of spirituality. To Melanie Hall, whose magical "God breeze" graces these pages and transforms my words into vibrant images, I offer my gratitude. —N.S.S.

This book is dedicated to the memory of my beloved mother and father, Sally Zaitchik Sohn and Nathan Raymond Sohn, with gratitude to them and to God for all the gifts of life.

And to the memory of one of those gifts—my beloved friend Janice Silverman.

—N.S.S.

For Kenny and Lori, our fellow sojourners in the sea of life.

—M.H.

*I*n the beginning, God created the heaven and the earth. And when the earth was almost done, God said, "Let Us make humans in Our image, after Our likeness."

To whom was God speaking? Who is "us"? Who else is included in the word "our"?

In the beginning,

God created the heaven and the earth

And the light
and the darkness.

And the waters and the land,
and the trees and the plants.

And the sun
and the moon
and the stars.

And the fish in the waters
and the birds in the sky.

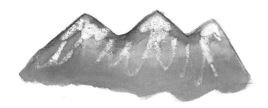

And all the wild creatures upon the earth.

And God saw that it was good.

But something was missing.

And God said, "Let Us make humans in Our image, after Our likeness…"

All the animals heard the words of God,
and they gathered together in the sunshine,
among the trees and the plants and all that
God had created.

"Are You speaking to us?" they asked.

And God said, "Yes. I am speaking to ALL that I have created. Man and woman shall be a part of nature, like each of you. And nature shall also be a part of them. Let Us give Our gifts to woman and to man, for in Our image will I make them."

The sun and the moon and the stars sparkled with excitement.

The waters shimmered and the earth quivered with anticipation.

The birth of humankind!

13

The animals were especially excited to
be included in this important moment.
They each thought about which gift
they could give so they would always be
connected to man and to woman.

"Make them brave," said the tiger.

"Make them gentle," said the lamb.

"Make them loud," roared the lion.

"Make them quiet," hushed the clam.

"Make them small," said the ant.

"Make them large," called the whale.

"Make them fast," snapped the cheetah.

"Make…them…slow," drawled the snail.

"Make them lazy," yawned the lizard.

"Keep them busy," buzzed the bee.

Then the swan spoke, very softly.
"Make them graceful, just like me."

One after another, all of the animals shared their ideas for how to make man and woman in their image.

The chimpanzee chattered,
"Let them always be curious."

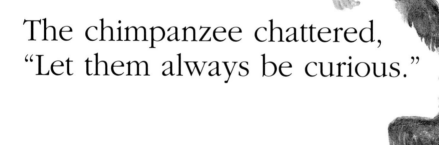

The ostrich bent low.
"Let them mind their
own business."

lazy

busy

graceful

The giraffe simply smiled, as it held its head high.

"Let them swim," said the fish.

The birds chirped, "Let them fly."

And God said, "They'll have to figure that one out for themselves."

The eagle said, "Then let them soar on wings."

And the nightingale sang,
"Give them voices that sing."

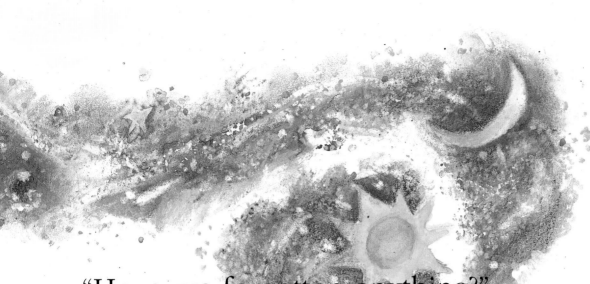

"Have we forgotten anything?"
asked the elephant.

"Good hearing," said the owl.

"Good vision," said the hawk.

"Playfulness," laughed the dolphin.

"Good appetite," gulped the shark.

All of creation became involved,
offering their gifts to humankind.

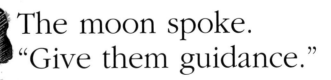

The moon spoke.
"Give them guidance."

The sun shone.
"Give them warmth."

The stars sparkled.
"Give them wonder."

The trees stood tall.
"Give them strength."

23

God thanked all of creation for their gifts.

And God said, "Behold. Woman and man shall fill the earth and have dominion over the fish of the sea, and over the birds of the air, and over every living thing that creeps upon the earth."

And all the animals gasped, and fled in fright, and hid behind the shivering trees.

"What will become of us?" they cried.

God calmed them and said, "Do not be afraid. For I will create man and woman in My image, after My likeness. Woman and man shall be partners with Me to care for you and all the world.

"In addition to *your* gifts, I will give them the gifts of goodness and kindness and love. I will bless them with the ability to understand and to reason, so they can choose between right and wrong. Just as you give to them, they will give to you."

The animals were no longer afraid. They came out from their hiding places and waited to see what God would create. And all of nature waited to see its reflection.

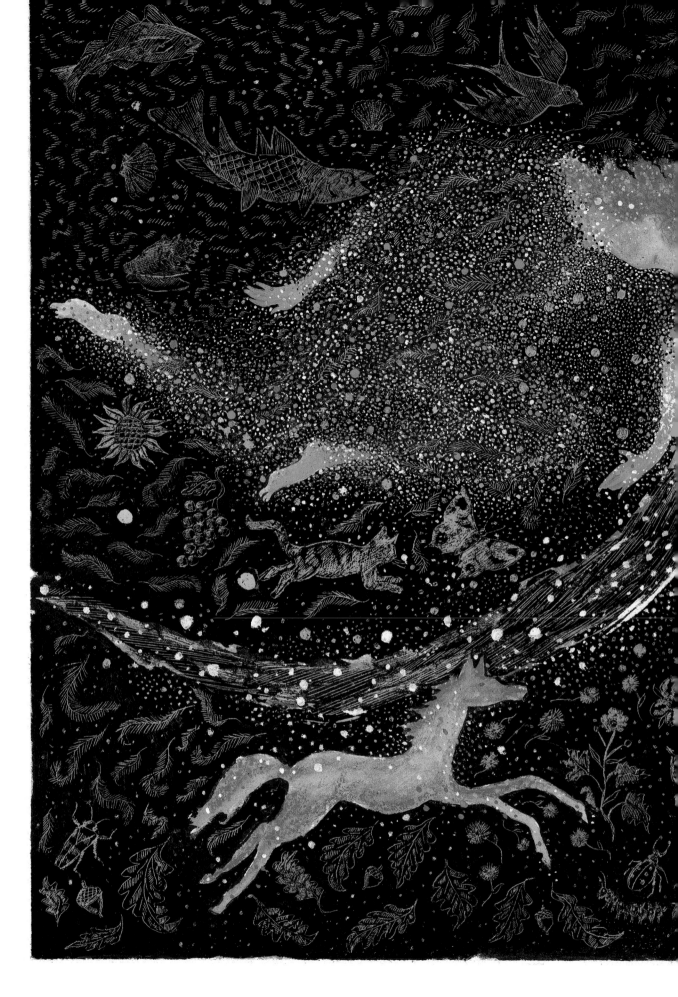

It was time. A mist appeared and watered the ground. Out of the dust of the earth, and with the breath of life…

God created man and woman.

In the image of God and in the image of all nature, God created them.

And nature lived in humankind.

And God saw that it was very good.